FARM BABIES

by
Joan Emerson

Scholastic Inc.

PHOTO CREDITS:

Photographs ©: CG Textures/David Edwards: cover background, 1 background; Dreamstime/Mazikab: 19; Fotosearch/Image Source: cover piglet eyes, 1 piglet eyes; Getty Images/Image Source: cover piglet, 1 piglet; iStockphoto: 8 (ddjunt), 16 (dgphotography), 10 and throughout (jcphoto), 15 (Johnboy-nz), 7 (KarelGallas), 4 inset and throughout, 6 and throughout (Kathryn8), 11 (LiuMeiLi), 24 (miskokordic), 3 (NikiTaxidisPhotography), 28 (Rehlik); Shutterstock, Inc.: back cover, 20 (Ana Gram), 23 (Eduard Kyslynskyy), 27 (hasrullnizam), 31 (Milosz_G), 12 (Wouter Tolenaars); Thinkstock: 4 main (anopdesignstock).

ISBN 978-0-545-80683-1

10 9 8 7 6 5 4 3 2 1   15 16 17 18 19/0

Printed in China   68
First printing, January 2015

Designer: Marissa Asuncion
Photo Editor: Amla Sanghvi

INTRODUCTION

Some animals live in the wild and some live on farms. Turn the page to meet some of the cutest animal babies from farms around the world!

PIGLETS

Baby pigs are called piglets. When a female pig gives birth, all the newborn piglets together are called a **litter**. In a litter there might be as many as 8 to 12 piglets! It is often said that pigs are dirty, smelly, and sweaty. In fact, pigs are actually fairly clean animals, and they cannot sweat at all!

Pigs can smell odors
5 to 7 miles away!

SHEEP

A young sheep is called a lamb. Sheep and their lambs live together in a group called a flock. Sheep have 360-degree vision. This means that a sheep can see all around without having to turn its head. This ability comes in handy for curious lambs!

In times of danger, sheep huddle close together to protect their lambs.

CHICKEN

Chickens are everywhere! Did you know that today there are more chickens alive in the world than any other bird **species**? Where do all these chickens come from? A mother chicken, called a hen, lays an egg and then sits on it for three weeks until it hatches. At that time, a little chick pecks its way out of the shell!

> When a rooster wants to impress a hen, he dances, makes lots of sounds, and picks up food from the ground with his beak.

SHEEPDOG

A sheepdog can be a farmer's great little helper. Sheepdogs love to **herd** other animals. By running back and forth around a group of cattle or sheep, they are able to control where the animals walk. This is how the sheepdog guides them in the right direction.

A sheepdog's fur is so long, it can take hours to brush through!

BARN CAT

Barn cats are hard workers that do a very important job on the farm. They catch mice and rats that might try to eat a farmer's **crops**. Barn cats spend a lot of the day outdoors, and sleep at night in the barn. Female barn cats give birth to kittens and teach them to become good hunters and farm helpers.

It is believed that humans have kept cats as pets since 7500 BCE!

LLAMA

Llamas are members of the camel family. Mother llamas snuggle close to their baby llamas, called crias, to keep them warm. Llamas are known for their soft and cozy wool. As a cria grows, its fur grows too!

Llamas have long, banana-shaped ears!

COW

There are about 9 million cows living on farms in the United States. A baby cow, called a calf, drinks milk from its mother until it is eight weeks old. As it grows, the calf will eat 40 pounds of food a day, including **cud**. Cud is food that the cow has already eaten and stored inside its stomach for later!

One cow can produce up to 400 glasses of milk per day!

CAMEL

Camels are famous for their hump, but they aren't born with it! As a camel calf grows, it eats grass, wheat, and oats. Soon, it develops the hump, which is a store of fat. (The hump does not hold water, as people once believed.) It can use this fat for energy when there is no other food to eat. A camel can survive up to 6 months without a meal!

When a camel gets angry, it spits a green, foul-smelling liquid all over its attacker!

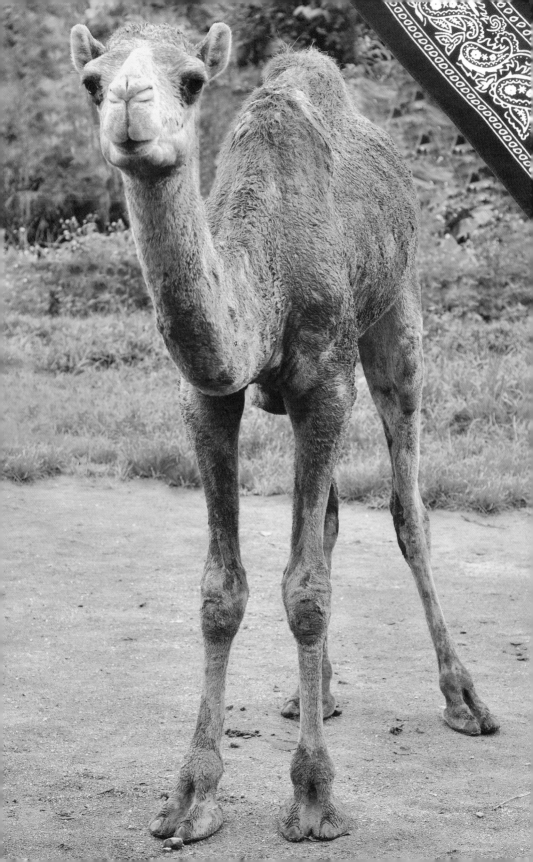

GOAT

A female goat is called a nanny. Her baby goat is called a kid—just like you! Nannies take good care of their kids while they grow. The kids are picky eaters. They will not eat any food that has touched the ground.

Both male *and* female goats have beards!

HORSE

When a female horse is born, she is called a filly. If a male horse is born, he is called a colt. Colts and fillies begin to stand and even walk only hours after birth! At that time, their legs are almost as long as they will be when they're fully grown. Soon, they will use these legs to run as fast as 44 miles per hour. That's about the average driving speed limit!

Horses like to sleep standing up!

DONKEY

Donkeys help out on the farm in lots of ways. They help protect sheep, cows, and goats. They can hear danger from far away and use their loud voices to warn the other animals. Donkeys also make great friends for horses. Donkey babies, called foals, learn how to help farmers just like their parents do.

Donkeys make a loud sound called a bray, which can be heard from over one mile away!

RABBIT

A baby rabbit, called a kit, is born hairless and blind. Soon, the kit grows a soft coat of fur and begins to see. As it grows, the kit will have an amazing sense of sight. A rabbit can see almost 360 degrees without turning its head. The only place it cannot see is right in front of its nose!

A rabbit can run up to 18 miles per hour!

TURKEY

Female turkeys, called hens, give birth to poults. Hens make great mothers. At night, poults sleep under their mother's wings for warmth. This **behavior** is called brooding. Many people think turkeys cannot fly. In fact, after only one month of life, wild poults can fly high enough to sleep in trees.

Turkeys have excellent vision, so it's very hard to sneak up on them!

ALPACAS

Alpacas are members of the camel family, but they look different from camels! Baby alpacas, called crias, are born covered in hair. Within one hour of their birth, crias can stand and walk. Soon, they use their strong legs to jump in the air and **arch** their backs in a dance called spronging. Their hair is called fiber, and it is very soft. It's even fireproof and waterproof!

Alpacas hum to their unborn cria. When a cria is born, he can recognize his mother's voice!

GLOSSARY

arch: something that has a curved shape

behavior: the way someone acts, either typically or in a particular situation

crops: plants grown for food for people or animals

cud: food that some animals, such as cows and sheep, bring up from the first part of their stomachs to chew again

herd: to move people or animals together in a group

litter: a number of baby animals that are born at the same time to the same mother

species: one of the groups into which animals and plants of the same genus are divided